Terrain Vague

Winner of the Verse Prize

Selected by Tomaz Salamun

Terrain Vague

Poems by

Richard Meier

Verse Press

Athens, GA · Amherst, MA

Library of Congress Cataloging-in-Publication Data
Meier, Richard, 1966–
 Terrain vague / Richard Meier.–– 1st ed.
    p. cm.
 ISBN 0-9703672-1-X (pbk. : alk. paper)
 I. Title.
 PS3563.E3459 T47 2000
 811'.54––dc21
                                        00-011568

The text of this book is set in Ehrhardt

Design by Brian Henry

Printed in the United States of America

9 8 7 6 5 4 3 2 1

FIRST EDITION

www.versepress.org

For Karen Volkman,
incomparable presence

ACKNOWLEDGMENTS

Thanks to the editors of the following magazines in which
these poems, in sometimes earlier versions, have appeared:

The Alembic: "Yellowstone"
American Letters & Commentary: "Seesaw Under Pine
   Shadows"
American Poetry Review: "Teary Erotic"
Another Chicago Magazine: "A Year Without Speaking,"
   "Study for an Antibiography"
Barrow Street: "This Animal"
Boston Review: "Correct Mistake"
Chelsea: "From the Kingdom," "Untitled Poem"
Fence: "Apology for the Birds"
Hanging Loose: "Battery Mate"
The Hat: "Direct Democracy"
LIT: "Dear Letter," "Dear, Reader," "Generalative"
Mudfish: "Her Florida"
o-blek: "False Spring"
The Paris Review: "Bayshore," "Obvious Doubles,"
   "Products, Promises"
Phoebe: "Effusive Trees"
Slope: "Closest of Shoes," "Ordering Order," "Our Parasol
   of Clouds," "Tacking," "Tipping Point," "Whose"
Verse: "*Beautiful*," "Done," "Gorgeous," "Nonplussed,"
   "Terrain *Vague*"
Western Humanities Review: "To Winter" "Trouble with the
   Sun"

Thanks also to Blue Mountain Center, The Millay Colony,
Vermont Studio Center, and Virginia Center for the
Creative Arts for the time and space to complete some of
these poems.

With gratitude to Carl and Carolyn Meier for the start and
support.

CONTENTS

I

II

III

First, we loved well and faithfully,
yet knew not what wee lov'd, nor why, . . .
—John Donne

I

OBVIOUS DOUBLES

Aeneas ditched Dido despite foundations. He had a vision.
Days he was frantic for explanation, nights
the fervid gods assailed him. Who knows the mind
of another? One dawn he found anticipation

was his mate, salt wind embraced,
while her house dwindled.
Only then did it feel like waking.
Never, nothing. What could he have told her?

Dido stacked the pyre, set the sword,
finding her dream in delirium.
I miss my love as well, my Aeneas,
her broad back turning, committing

its nightly division, shifting from questions
of love, from searching caresses.
Swift foundation, prow of a ship
whose course reveals the sea's

white rollers, rushing, rushing, unsubsiding, a pair of
    lovers
not returning (such are lovers) to the sea's green whisper.
(She the lonely figure at the head and we
the doubled sea. O paradox!)

Dido ended in Hades, never understanding
will's failure, spun halfway on her heel
and ran, so all that flickering landscape lacked
the vision of perfidious Aeneas. But you,

conflicted Aeneas, cyclic stone, constant sea,
make of your back, unbroken flesh, a queer commitment,
that absence embodied is different,
that its shifts aren't loss.

GORGEOUS

Final, like a score
her slouch pronounces,

announcing death's half-touching conclusion,
half-death and half-touching,

the trees between winter and spring,
unsynchronized green, barren, and bud.

There is a story of the brother, infant by the pool,
rescued, revived by a blow, the tiny body an island

awash in sun, not part of the world.
Now the wet streets and brightened leaves

release an odor of chlorine, poison and alive.
The mourners were celebrant, are.

Our love is alive is the chorus,
an invitation she takes from teeth clenched

enamel against enamel against idyll, cold pastoral
traded up for an uncomforting faith.

It's the baby dropped in the pool's blue bowl won't
    breathe.
It's the sun will light a scene, the sun will dry a stain.

It's a vow if the infant, grown, far gone, cannot remember
black spots like birds, brought on by a lack, the concrete
    white,

the water what color and green like a bruise,
to hold the stopped, slick chest, and call it back by force.

DIRECT DEMOCRACY

Big clouds like disappointing hats
drift and disenfranchise the only stance you've got.
The stork waits to strike its place
in heaven from the lake as an example

I'd prefer to be eating, get on with the digesting,
which spreads in rings until interrupted
by the sand that's trucked in hourly with a resulting
planetary affluence too human, unnerving.

But that was in the past of the alternate, while this
still needs some preparation. A tornado in our old
        hometown
has torn the middle of the artificial meadow.
Proposing bounds is natural practice. The roof of folly

is money, though, repairs. Once below the clouds has
        settled
for a spate of sticks atop a concrete pole,
the stork unburdened is a vow of silence.
The vote at last was to over-ride limits.

The wolves re-introduced themselves, subcutaneously,
the play bow best-of-all-universal, but I couldn't
        remember
my face, was it before or after they had eaten the stork?
Society agreed there. A grieving not made to save her.

TACKING

We couldn't find the coffin,
like a boat that had drifted.
We drifted before she died,

on the boat with the woman who died.
It seemed to us like drifting, seaward
breeze singing, a zig-zag from open to open.

Her curse for the shore, she captained. A common
maneuver. We learn later.
So when we had had it

the coffin was polished,
sealed white like the boat's outer hull,
inner curve of a shell. An inside and outside.

Then not lost and we'd lost it.
Charlene, what a strange woods we'd arrived in,
a bright day almost to the middle,

your sense of destination, my second confusion,
and nothing to be seen. The signal lights foundered
in a green sun. The brothers years

after building boats.

HISTORY TOWN

Shipyards and widow's walks abandoned
as if death had eloped with devotion
on a South Seas voyage.

In such a town the people are ecstatic, bound
by nothing in the presence of tradition,
a selling point we've all agreed on.

The Puritans chose it by accident,
or it chose them. Cancel all our appointments
with destiny and chance.

We're students of history
fighting to preserve the century-
cracked masts half-sunk in the shallow harbor,

the ones that never came to use.
And the milk bottles broken on the rocks,
once filled from local heifers,

cream like whitecaps on the top.
The ocean used to live here too.
We see it sometimes in our dreams.

TERRAIN *VAGUE*

The stunted pines elude capture
in a thousand sidetracked increments.
The wind will never understand them.
Like us it is forced to go on

the trail that only seems to wind
and has all the straightness of water,
the holes in the stones speak, a tale of crevice,
and arrives without desire at the sea.

The red buoy marks a diver,
the red forehead where I tried to enter,
and the birds are gaps in a terra cotta roof,
discovered in abandon, the black hole

blimped above the white of island,
fences and exits, an ad hominem for language,
hand-held constants.
The ships don't cross the horizon, the direction

given is sideways, and our cynic
proof misses disappearance. The cliff face
throws itself upon the bay of azure,
a backwards red attempt at sunset,

while the night sneaks up behind us,
an emptiness, high-beamed and ceilinged,
the house where one is living.
Space circles

like the wolf I called out to you,
our movement must be less,
then undetectable. Birds and planes fly below us,
lovers urge the dwelling off the Earth,

what thought belongs to?
falling onto so much wreckage,
the fatal cushion. The bed one wakes is tilted
rack unto the sun.

GOING TO BE

Missing the bus was how it expressed itself
on me, the sun on me, and the bus missed

both as itself and the expression of the split
world where I wasn't when I chose to be

here, on the floor, in a tipped square of sun, a skin,
or missing the bus on the bus, the bus of the room

without me in it, the woman alone at the table with a
    book,
the mother, the room a missed bus when I left it, a
    cigarette

smoked or not, to be smoke or cigarette.
I tried to decide it so the bus wouldn't pass

or I'd be on it without the room missing
but I couldn't decide it. In my mind it wasn't

made up. My sympathies divided. A tipped square of sun,
or the bus moving through the sun's shapelessness,

a chariot of sun, the sun squared, a tipped square and
    shapeless,
the other square of the sun's chariot, a displacement,

of the sun rising in metal over the body
like water, proportionate, displaced. I divided,

this was what was being ghosted.
The floor stayed warm where the ghost had left it.

On the missing bus I couldn't speak. Don't sit with me I
said.
And so I sat tentative to the seat, the thought, and the
missed bus.

I wasn't on it.
On was going to be difficult.

CORRECT MISTAKE

Like Frankenstein the monster I willed you wake
who was really—correct mistake—doctor and monster.
But you played dead, seemed sadist, wielding that
    penultimate,
human, a moment, gone, or still in bed.

The wind offered rattled windows and blown-off
    blossoms,
the intimacy of an eye that looks protected, vanity,
a windy brain that plumbs the surface,
the body's fool-hardiness

displayed in apple petals laid deathless,
detached, presentable, feelingless,
snow not melting into union, oh eventually
rotten, forgotten: it's blood I shriveled from, its secret

courses inside you. The nightmare, my dream
mask of discharged blood, love's misprize, a masque
of the moment it wasn't you, mere token,
my stacked heads totem, the latest too-late acquisition.

The vita of the tree stays hidden
from the wind's ravish. So yield my ghost
control, unman that manikin, and you will awaken
into union, my imagined monumental moment?

I forget too scientistic, familiar failure of the alchemist:
gold stuck in head. The unpredicted follows its
    unprediction

like the clock's arrhythmia advances the hours
to a dead certainty. A loan is a hole and any gravedigger

gardener knows the dirt alone won't fill it.
My inhabit of waiting, buds borrowed from the branches,
it can't be forgiven. The years I dun against add-up,
yield dead already us.

FALSE SPRING

Life was not expected here.
The almanac warned of fluctuations
and now summer's been exposed
in this erosion of winter. Forsythia

bloom pale as butter, the past's dinner
on a rotting table, pleasure suddenly
alive in its shallow grave. It's false
spring and shall we fear

eternity or its stubborn instants? Is it
the birds singing or ourselves? This bush
burning out of season we can be certain
belongs to no one. That was the warning.

The seasons just aren't themselves these days.
And the past, with all its children,
seems disfigured. The order matters.
We choose to name

each yellow blossom false beneath the brevity-
dizzy weight.

STUDY FOR AN ANTIBIOGRAPHY

She's had a thousand operations, corrective, as if
the revenge of a dozen archeologied classes.
The point of expertly flaked flint unburied itself,
brief excerpt from the memoir of a late
twentieth century spine. The human
race is derived by such attack. History
has its ape (theory), however physical. The surfaced bone
expresses the river's sediments. Eons of flow. I was
    mistaken
for my own fossil, if you can believe that.
"We only intended to study the dead," they said.
The site of the shopping center just happened
to deprive these bones, and feelings (a sign
of life against the wind blows). Discernment
wasn't, as easily suspected. Transparencies peeled away
on the other hand the skin and skeleton
inviolately. Display of brain changes
against a western window. Just light,
you see. It, the subject, walks the earth,
a heightened sensitivity. We ask ourselves, can you
describe these invisibles that torment? like a who's-the-
    primitive
narrative hitting on a nerve. The guy's a Neanderthal. A
    broken tongue
depressor probes scattered centers. Dull or sharp at each
    prick,
please. The raw edge coupled with the doctoral
words. Universal experience.
I'm guilty of it here as my inheritance.
An oral of my deepest sympathy, i.e. blood

that boils at the sight of, or the tongue impressed.
That all we've got.

BAYSHORE

Let's lie here for a moment and talk.

The pristine path describes the borders
of a farm abandoned, reserved
as a letter from the loved
no longer and no longer known.

The blossoms, and there are hundreds,
carry each a touch of salt.
The wind, with its million proofs,
tossed them into our path.

We don't have to say the body breaks.
In the sun by the bay,
it lays broken on the granite.
The circular path doesn't beckon.

It's legislated. So five minutes is a lifetime,
the slap and regroup of the tide
throwing its weight to the shine and sultry air.
Salt and slight, a pressure

on the warmed skin, a pleasure
on what is not built—
words our mouths feel,
not obliged to make—to heal entirely.
We love this,

                  how it shatters and gathers,
white and rainbow spume

to the dull pea-green of home.
In the afternoon sun, a lifetime, a lull—

O on our throne we cannot.

DONE

Once you heard
a self escape, a crisis of leaves
stained the blue slate walk, a clatter of heels
rang the new tarred street,

your own tearing out of earshot.
You went on without, the suburb at night
just that, a sprawl below
the faint rumor of a brilliant center,

where the wind was a passing car
rattling the leaves, where the leaves were raked
in humps at evening burned. When is it life
became literal, an injury

that one lives with at the end
of a long duplicity, where blame is evident
in the sprawled body, and the wondering
is how to praise, to live without that burden?

ABSTRACT

Sites boasted ghosts beside the green van they slept in—
    written
they instead of us, to make it history, a moment
when every soul in America slumbered.

The vantage points sprang pre-ordained, pulled into.
A sign pointed past nothing to fight for,
where men had disappeared into, unpursued through,

impenetrable canyons, Badlands, one of many attractions
requiring patience. The burros grown wild, wiry-haired,
beside sage-brush and cactus, road-bed, our burdens

abstracted, upon them. The mountain was rendered,
after decades of blasting,
a horse for the generations, crazy, deracinated.

The Great Salt Lake stretched shallow as accident.
The wading was one labor, the sunset another,
the lack of intervention, where the son and the mother

stood mistaken as sisters, between back-lit cumulus
and a water that wouldn't take them.
The horizon was splintered

by mountains, for days with nothing between them.
Hands left the wheel, eyes drifted to prairie, a cabin
where the wind names

the chinks in the walls and had named them,
for years of insistence, the burden I give them,
a road straighter than accident.

WHAT ABOUT THE PSYCHIC LANDSCAPE?
I'M GLAD YOU ASKED . . .

A tree was trying to stand up inside of me,
across the street and through the window,
the limbs like a just-dropped giraffe's
desperate attempt on the savanna to assemble itself
into itself, and walk away.

The sphinx sweats. Then her skin pops off in chips.
What kind of day are you having, she said by saying
    nothing,
nose trick she'd learned from Napoleon's cannons
burning a trail into silence. The passageways suffer
from human breath. Perhaps it should be forbidden.

But who's whose monument? The local cathedral
offers the same losses, but I can't relate to it.
Its questions aren't going to be on my test,
and my personal tourism isn't interested.
The treeness that the tree has is entirely missing.

No choice, I say I believe. The trunk hasn't taken a step
but it's full of direction, the leaves whipping wildly
ever more civil branches. The bell tower rings
between the hours, getting into the swing of things,
a funky automation that may beat plague, co-opt defeat.

I tore off my left and right tits so I could love you
man to woman with my new flat chest.
Sphinx-like you fitted my cavities effortlessly,

banked that watery, no end of difference, in the art of not
    saying
just the right thing. Loving block of stone.

COUPLETS

A wall. The winter ivy greens morning and evening
    toward the middle
where is cut a single small window.

Dark, iridescent, the starling lives in the gable.
A hole in the shelter. A shelter.

I'm told she is regal, unable to speak, the hair pulled back
    silver
in a new severity, revealing a native beauty, that we'd
    never known her.

Buds bury the winter, our fondest imaginings.
The tree does not betray its strain. Fruit, the blossoms.

OUR PARASOL OF CLOUDS

From the air we reeled
her where light as a tree she floated.
Rooted in air, given up root.
The lost was light was
our dream's logic.

We thought, and we thought she had a root
in the Sunday sea, her historical,
the promenades in endless dresses,
imagined miles of petticoats, of which we reminded her.
Because if she was familiar, our parasol hour.

In that thought we could have her.
There wasn't a sky that I can remember
rather a white that held us together,
finial gauzes. The sea and sand were
fashioned. The sky unfolded.

Her presence was an argument
we made her, she against us. We felt her
unsteady, sandy skin. The wind scurried
around our ankles a cutting. Particular,
crowd. Her guise and distance.

Her comprehension, as I am recording,
was sand furrowed by the waves slipping—
our will the whitecaps splitting—
out of reach.
Her white head held our hands. Our root

dreamed in sand. Our thunderous our
constant we learned her
like the waves' dumb speech—she all the we
the sea couldn't enter into her—
white-wash reduced to whisper,

the beach the barrier.

CONFLICTING TESTIMONY

I'm hoping it's going to rain. The cows have to eat
next winter. The time spent
figuring out connections, a constellation
of shooting stars called incunabula, and dug for in the
    dirt . . .

But we don't feed the birds, we attract them,
fat as intangibles, to the glass part of our houses.
Their songs cannot contain complaint,
and a red that's more like strawberries than blood

is a theme of my motion picture, whose symbols are
    shattered,
whose moral is forget the birds above the battle
you've recreated in your consciousness,
and then forget that. The shepherd yields a real crook

and everyone wonders about owning a neck,
while her own is being, and the one that's fit.
But that's not right. No one had to breathe a word,
the black bird, was swallowed after light.

FROM THE KINGDOM

News of the death
then a bottle of ash.
You believed that leap.
And once thanked for participating . . .

The metaphor wept, art of the ancients,
power hired, knell clanged outside us,
recorded, inducted,
our tears felled inaccurate.

The yellow dog,
blind guide and honored primitive,
invited guest,
slept envied in harness.

Once you know it's a cry of distress
it's different. Loons keen
over motorboat.
I am inanimate then.

Comparisons
excruciate. Relief, like next weathers,
lies not in the seeking.
They're white as sea-shells now,

or any other fertilizer.
A cloud looks like something,
and then is someone else.
No questions asked.

EFFUSIVE TREES

These trees inflict their weeping on us,
Hunched and shuddering, losing their almond leaves
    today.
We felt nothing until the world made it so.
How long ago they taught us, and now review our sorrows
Demanding answers we can't think of, actions
That diminish us in our stand apart from all that,
Our small deliberate stand, wind-break and grove,
Sacred place and picnic spot, shade and light in perfect
    measure,
Apart from all the natural candor, the countless points of
    rain,
The whining wind that these past nights has had the
    building surrounded
The way the old man or woman inside you, beside you,
Mutters in the blind spot behind your ear. So you think
To ask a little of what's force fed, use the weight of the
    world
Against the world, like the master of an art of grace and
    violence,
To let the waterfall say all until the word trips off your
    tongue,
Expect lightning, Santa Ana, and Sirocco to deliver
Desire relentless and undeniable, knowing no bounds.
    And so it is
I walk smack into a sign, fall into the fountain, trip on a
    body
Of rags incorporated along the common mall, caught
    gawking

At the world whose trees weep
In wind, laughter, intolerable sadness.

IF WE WANT TO BE

You wound your eye down
to red and yellow
because it seemed monstrous
behind a mountain to precipitate your leaving.

It hung there burning
like the last thing
when really it was the only thing
in the whole scene going.

It wasn't even you.
It was spring in cold storage,
buds in suspension,
loose petals folded into buds.

Summer was strange without it.
The heat industrial and you lacking
you sent away, the safe-keeping,
a taste of metal never washed away.

Autumn delivered us into its keeping,
like the deliberation was made outside us.
The air was red and yellow; we kept an eye on.
The days began and reversed before their ending.

Of course there are decisions in which the seasons
and the heavens are only a part.
As it happens,
we decide what is happening.

That's what I lost,
though nothing was taken,
because nothing I had ever had was taken,
a personal red and a personal yellow.

We are not whole.
I don't know if I want to be.
The arrangement of things in a green, red and yellow
    circle
admits nothing.

SEARCH FOR DIGNITY

A tasteful blue behind night-flattened branches
belonging to the evening is impossible, to discern
to mean to offer your hand. The good news concusses
into not being someone,
replaying the scene in miniature. I prefer not to
to the school boy transfixed by the picture
of the man who holds the picture of the man
who holds the picture into wonder irreproachable,
shiver that rises through rubber and leather,
glitter of sand that is flush for the concrete,
the quartzing of movement, the moment a handful
of people are given
to understand without the need to be forgotten,
whatever that means. I have a collection of goats on
        packages,
and they have all escaped it.

Last night a long dream that continued in and out of several wakings. You were with another and did not meet me at the places and times we had appointed. And then I came across you on a sidewalk, walking, in your tan raincoat, in your black shirt. In that city by chance, and in that place, and in that time. The buildings curved around and the sidewalk expanded at your center, reapproachment through a fish-eyed lens. How unsurprised you were, the very softness of your hair resigned. In another room I pleaded to see you. You had retired upstairs with another. Was it true I had hit you? You were there and who wasn't. I grabbed you with my excess, a danger had passed, with nothing required. Once I'd held a stone, larger than I was, and meant the caress. And you held me calmly, nothing to be avoided, a burden like waking, welcomed though welcome is not what requires it. It consists beyond situation, and I won't name it down. Your eyes closed exactly as the day when mine will not open, so I saw that, and the shadow the eye-ridge casts on the eye.

We live on accident. The unlit lawn rolls down and the foot feels a gap to the lake where the stars are shaking and it's all uncharted, off course, excessive and serving my accuracy. I remember the dog shook her own head to return the room violently. Her cunt melted a blizzard in the Chinese poem, that old woman, saving a village. If it's true, please call me. I've wrapped arms around my head, or blanket around my arms. The embrace is accurate, the silence and mis-statement, the lamp spined, the lake of jostled stars, the stone in our places, respectively, all that's required, morning, shifting focus. The accurate insists after the words aren't available, and the cunt converses past the blizzard. The dream was an acute distortion, of we've held each other possibly, gazing into lids, always behind our backs.

APOLOGY FOR THE BIRDS

The jays, the cardinals on the vine,
the cough that starts inside the ear, the screech
that joins it like an orange pair
of cats that saunter toward a mirror kiss.
One is left to lick its whiskers in the grid
of summer's chair's uncushioned shadow,
casually, as if its solo post repose was
all- and after-image of the act. My hand was
taken and returned, unarmed, unharmed, the sergeant
won't accept the theft. The therapist understands you
to the extent your mother loved you, and again
that warmth coiled in a blanket, not to be awoken,
grows cranky when spoken to directly,
and thereby ceases like a candle's blown flame.
The rise of the ocean when the heart's held
beneath it. I cover my mouth, apologize for the birds.

II

TO WINTER

The garden's gone south
to another, the green body, though strangely
left its skeleton.
Bach on the stereo

plays the branches
and busted stalks through me
like a sinew thread threading
the needle eye awled

in a primitive bone—
my capacity, that carnivore
fellow feeling, fattening
as the squirrel eats itself into winter.

Armored in high notes and coat
of brittle links cinched
together, I face the wind as a devil,
determining all that does not love me.

What a powdered wig the sky wears.
What a Great Chair I prop in,
a feather to comfort and raise me up,
an ark to avenge my stature.

The last rose told long ago
to get about its business loiters.
Who's on this beat? or it says,
I'll die on his vine.

Led to believe the note struck familiar
as the branch suffers my greenstick fracture.
I got a vulgar reason, got got at,
sad and vulgar, a bargain price.

But the birds pick-up the fugue
like pallbearers in plague time, an intimacy
assumed in my delivery, why disguise,
beautiful as it cannot be refused?

LIE FOR EVERYTHING

First I reading *Crime and Punishment* and second I
    reading
that there you had been unfaithful to me and ancient
by newspaper standards it was, would be
left over brittle and the packing
in a box of oranges, the oranges themselves seen spinning
like planets, elongated, assuming the natural imperfect
proportion of the spherical in a spinning,
gravitated reel, it seemed at that moment, when the world
    was mine
more than ever
and seemed to be spinning, the spun knotted boards of
    the floor
as I felt I spinning further
it must have been because the world is always
spinning and felt still, less or further
my own indecision like a current resisted, a hand shoved
    up it
returns nothing of the river to its origin, the mounting
ploughed green an allusion to semi-permanence. Unfaithful
    meaning

had not faith in faith in me, or in you had, or in you you
found another faithful, to you twice faithful, me, a sense
    of opinion
pervades an article discarded
about the rising floodwater in the plains
disguised as analysis disguised as news
pure event that is presented as God becomes a pool of blood

that dead yet creeps across the floor and seeps between its
    rough
cut pages. Despite I sleep. Despite the room
I cannot see insists, insists
unreasonably what next step, what to be taken
more like R. or S. in terms of the novel, unfaithful to the
    author
unfeeling Fyodor Dostoevski. Between them I
went back, went forth.
What of the horse whose eyes were beaten?
What of the horse that planted its hoof above M.'s heart?
A yellow bruise in the shape of a hoof, a misshape of the
    sun.

It was common as I had a sense, like the house
painter who confesses, this game like that, like that
that is unfaithful to you is an event that I have taken
like the line about a jewel, unnoted, though I don't know
I love you the way infidelity is untrue
and the truth wanders on without the jewels
the bloodstained purse a statement that questions itself
    into silence
where love does not submit to it like the river
beside a building hacked up into smaller and smaller
    apartments
a blanket strung across a corner, the river laid between us
and the novel between us
the articles of faith strewn about the bedchamber
are articles, the terrible false expressions of the buttons.

The room doesn't stop sweating, or the body.
I know can be seen not looking like a horse
in blinders or the tree in spring that eyes you with green lids

a yellow light pours through and finds you.
Are they in love with the sun? What is left? What is leaving?
The horses are the ones that turn the world, the pair of
        horses.
They are named with tongues and must be repeated.
The river is beneath them.
They stand for nothing.

DEAR, READER

The wall is taken
down as far as glass
because the place for it exists.

To watch the angle
we erred into the linden
read the sun and straighten, ask where

the word exists, that I could write it and correct
you of my perspective
which sees the sun down also.

I want to say it straightest
the line involves the curve and beds
distortion. Best, better to remind me.

EXCLAIMED

The artist of another generation
who arrived without a head and added,
my study sympathizes
you as equally.

A gesture never matched a body.
One or the other seems palsied,
the collar stiffened by another era,
the hand too slurred, or the lip too spoken.

In the photograph where a grey felt
hat becomes the head, the queer
of we don't wear them, is a history of feeling.
The edges where I see him,

a man dies despite the questions.
Suffering doesn't want itself,
looks elsewhere.
The hole is it that gives,

and the song that needs opening?
The dead exclaimed Orpheus.

A YEAR WITHOUT SPEAKING

At the bus stop we had a year without speaking.
I wonder if the other person still has it
like I do. I use it
against the sky or at a cocktail party it's so long
nothing can see through its nothing
the false comfort of a month you can't remember
a scarf the size of a hamlet or something made monastic
after the fact tripping on an empty street and cursing and
    suddenly stopping cursing
to embarrass your ghost and the grit
or a country that reifies the injustice done to it
into a formidable wall of China in their people's
heads polished toward the bronze or alabaster
like we all kept taking buckets from the oceans until
    someone joked
leave some for the fishes
and it was all back where it started
the weapon is that nothing ever happened or so little
and for such a string of days
the saints fasted
we're led to believe because of an out-sized hunger and
    energy
a paradox like Homer or Emily Dickinson
can be terrifying admiring
ivied bricks on the way to the grocery store for an avocado
or a woman who catches in her sob till she's past you
and then on those occasions I choke on my silence for the
    reassurance
like a head held under water for longer and longer intervals
against the incidence of torture

though the count is scored in the head also
and if she doesn't have it where is it and under what
    circumstances
we'd stop again in that shadow.

Though we had met a year or two later
I left it out not to shade the ending too early
because it wasn't called for as though it had to be
at a dance or by water and she like a beaten
opponent said why did you hate me
and my denial was a false banner
of it never happened exactly like the silence
was someone else's prediction
like naming in the poem her Cassandra
an ancient history acquiesced to as the sob
I turned to see released was released I released it.

SEESAW UNDER PINE SHADOWS

It doesn't illustrate. The chickadee,
black-helmeted,
takes a bath in the face of lack, of interest.
The foible was moving through a landscape

with a scanner, as the eye is estimated,
never having held or bitten.
The scar that binds the body
suborns it to it, the green of the cardinal

against the dull, red, thump of the overgrowth.
A purpose is served in a passive voice,
a trickle of thought against the ice
necessary and not the orange

and black of an oriole bathing
once in a lifetime of waiting
to enter through its zero and undistinguished
eye to some hump or cameled. The fullness

surprises, dropped over vision,
a hood before the eyes get lined.
The thicket's been receded,
inside us stands whoseless, sightless red and orange,

past collision.
The eye escapes in open, through the hole
draws us against a sun unchanged.
The fact flicks a feather. The flick flickers.

NONPLUSSED

Longing for a storm again to steal
a little of this agency. Dante the divine
detective of has got a mountain
to can't need it. I've an in
between, a canyon's shaking, for the essential
part of it is missing. So what
to mount the search with, or for,
for that displacement. A cavity can lure
its opposite, fulfillment, and if the flash
flood were the canyon
we had hope to be delivered, dead belly
of the whale alive with fishes, or a God
who chased, thus to replace, replenished us?

TEARY EROTIC

The covering has been blown from the body
and the tears tumbling down the wreckage I lick
without wanting to know, just wanting, that order
of knowledge, like shimmying

into the shimmer of a thousand suns,
tongue I thought eliding tears, the year of waste
with a taste of sweat and sexual fluid,
warmth against a situation, an afternoon so bitter
it revives, wind an adrenal needle
in winter's arrested heart.

Later, together, one heads for the movies,
slow steps past spectacular dogwoods,
blossoms white, undeniably
like an explosion, an affront to the personal,
the raw, archaic cold.

Yet one doesn't know how to hate the world
in its lockstep and disregard.

Unfragile petals, fraught wind.

To this day
the psalm-singer mutters through the desert
so long past answer
the parched air answers
once less than the dry lungs sing.
Lover who left me I intended so

to sing to your not listening,
of radioactive ash shipped back to Bikini,
as a mockery, an ironic
catharsis of our present situation,
a plea,
and still it was income for the islanders
coming again, *changed to the changed lagoon*,
the enemy won over by a handing
out of t-shirts, a confusion of invitations
to dive by the wreck, perfect
for coral in the latest sumptuous twist.

O economy
of innocence for guilt for extravagant beauty . . .
an erotic
started in the sub-atomic
ends in a tear that made it
over the breasts and belly to the sex.

How to hate the world
of bombshells on the naked beach,
the nearly naked body?
The loved, lost, loses shape
like the diver flying underwater.

Redemption, as the fused beaches
are beautiful, the lagoon
aglow with chemicals and phosphorescent life.

NATURAL

A storm builds a house to live in,
of shorn moments shingled, walls of wrack
and the self sheltered, bereft in a particular
uplift of leaves suddenly rooted
in the veins of their tree. I miss you
blows insignificant in multiple, the sentimental
scattered in the elemental, rain
seeding the cracks with a sentiment
refreshed, loss a wash
no one had to leave one for.
No more sense waiting for the weather than.
A limb in shifting aspect means one thing.
Ironically it was yesterday I grabbed the push
broom impetuously and swept the path.
As if it required a precedent.
Moses had a good day at the Red Sea,
coinciding with the tide, the glamour
and stink of the bared flats
so seemed an answer it was
other. You're natural as a two-lane highway.
Which isn't to discount the common
summer rains that fall into themselves so swiftly,
a pall on the face of their cloud,
the air remains unwanted
flesh in a self-indulgent sun.

BEAUTIFUL

Fall's lured buds blast twigs,
and the blooms pick locks in lousy wigs
of dead, disguising,
wish-bone needle clusters
high pine fallen. Fuck,

that's not organized where I come from,
where no-see-ums have a summer name, and steal it,
where we give it a rest. And here's where I said
I was knowing you were going

into past. I mean that shit is *tight*.
Girls within girls without flowers,
demetered inner clock dropped down a hole.
That ragged white and purple is so untrue

intones a giant running backward
feels alive because he's less gigantic, coaxing
the skinny wrist-sequoia from the paper.
I donate my front door to science.

SLIPPER

The fear in the stones dragged
shaking to the sea that smoothed them,
the falseness in that
fear giving rise to another. Home requires
always a decision.
The saint wants the love of imposition
and you stare at it strangely, reduced to.
You see how difficult a gift is,
never what's given, the need not to release,
and the change that overcomes it.
White flowers that said forbidden
or death prophecy in lilies,
who'd wanted to receive them?
And rightly it is the hand that trembles,
bones and joinings hidden, that holds the offer,
the god it needs to take,
and the not to see what's missing.

ORDERING ORDER

Windshield wiper fluid, buy a house,
the total conception is the sister
beats the toddler weeps
the mother scolds the sister whines
the baby screams *in wonder*
now tell me is that naturally
normal, or unnaturally natural, you who stripped for
    nature (me),
too qualified to judge, likewise lack of bodkin. Thinking
of discipline
isn't, any more than your own bitter
end, or theirs, or this's
is inured by the insurance. I never handed in. The sun
    shines up
and under the haze we feel so hemmed
and blue-white in, as in the hound
the eyes empyrean blue and cream
staring undisturbed by pupil
stopped us, not him, from seeing.
What to make of proved a good dog also?

UNTITLED POEM

How to say it
I don't feel like Odysseus
or Telemachus Not Penelope or Achilles
Not the unbent bow Not the abused Cyclops
I feel like the tapestry I feel Penelope
over me in the twentieth century
the shuttle shot and the loom clanking
a scene in the morning a scene in the evening
My father is not the herdsman or the father
sleeping under hides in the herdsman's hut
My mother the sheep and my father the wool
The dye and the berry
The scene's like a pendulum
The earth turns and time passes and the pendulum
     swings straight
as an exhibit at the Museum of Science
But I'm not the scene I'm the earth turning
boars in the wood and bronze-headed spears
My father the warp and my mother the woof
I feel like the delaying that for Penelope is living
expressed in a tapestry
and does she finish it ever no
I think she is done with weaving
Penelope O Penelope
Odysseus My Odysseus
What do they care what I feel
Nothing, the tapestry is passed off successfully as finality
is done and undone as hope

BATTERY MATE

A cabal of crows and church bells. Good morning.
Cacophony? It's all foreign to me. No sugar,
and a lot of milk. No answer. The demand
plays on. Why angels love time
is they embody the end of it.
The crows are a life-scheme
if fathomed, living long
on leavings. Saunter off the freeway
in their pick of time. The angels don't
get nervous not being human.
The ballplayers do, sweat pooled
below Valenzuala's eyes,
whose age is indeterminate and controversial,
like a beautiful martyr's. He no longer
glances heavensward in motion
but locks on his battery mate's deliberately
out of scale left hand. You're right,
both bells and birds have stopped.

III

TIPPING POINT

The car ran backward down the street.
Eventually came in on a horse, like a god kept going.
In his absence the ravens dominate with calls of
cause the little birds fear, and their makers,
knowing the past now is everything the tar pit
said it was, e.g. beautifully preserved bones
and thanks to the absence of oxygen. The orange walls of
    the hospital
had us feeling a little sick on the edge of our seats,
the clumsy depiction of the violence getting to our hearts.
It was just the way we would have done it, backyarded,
the sheets torn from the beds of our neighbors
as our own, only to have it end up filed
down in the basement with the fear of human contact.
To be living in those times when a bare leg's gray hairs
write your screams into the concrete. The soul bears a
    double imprint
is the point they match to both your leather feet.

PARTICLES AND SPECTRES

Under the influence of the underworld setting,
mood already depressed and all others sleeping,
heads like dead tulips drooping
in the train's now infernal seeming rhythms.
Such crackpot symmetry cracks a smile,

your refusal a mile down the street regardless
of appearances to disappear. The gregarious-
to-the-point-of-dementia man with the moustache
meets a woman night after night
at top of the stop's dank stairs, the stars

are out, they seem befuddled
by their devotion, or annoyed, they're thinking
death was never meant to be like this, we all go like this,
briskly through the spiked black turnstile,
shuffling up into an unexpected light

we'd been told to believe in at the end, an atmosphere
where ordinary clouds scud
exhilarations of disaster: we'd forgotten so quickly, reaching
for the rain-soaked leaves, counting the illuminated
bridges on one noticeably blood-filled hand.

The air is potent and the nose breathes hard:
it must belong to us. Have we been dying
for so long? Our eyes feel fresh cut,
drinking it all in. And so it is:
a thousand deaths, and then a countless number.

Butterfly against the gray Atlantic,
cormorant stalking the blue Pacific.
Impacted star
whose salt-sized grain pins a hole to our chests.
Light's let in.

What we don't believe means nothing.
Yesterday and tomorrow
draw contracts on our fate. Which we
do we belong to? Love can't be avoided.
The street corner on the edge of the earth

holds these particles and spectres. These you.

YELLOWSTONE

At the end of our trail
a deer leg freshly severed.

The picnic in the parking lot
with our new corkscrew.

We pulled the cork to get
our instincts back.

What was destination
where the people took pictures of signs

framing out the sky?
and that bloody leg, even now,

proving, pulsing our distance.
A line of cars means bison

or the hot rotten river
littered with bathers.

We joined them and it stunk
like all the day's pleasures.

I am in remission officially,
like just above ground you whispering–

we slept on our numbered parcel–
that should have been our leg.

Only the pronoun seemed strange,
a slide of that vocation,

the bear visible, barely,
the singing ordered on the trail.

DEAR LETTER

The innocence you gave me on a platter I recognized,
the head that follows self into the river,
baptist, narcissus, thank you.
Your veils are green and fill the trees
in Tuscaloosa
where I see myself not seeing you
in the delicious caper of a rain that came and went
or comes and goes. The applause is famous.
The famously empty matter of the theatre
of the blood is bloodless, a bonfire of negatives
where the breath of the stars is taken
in great gulps to be returned, informed and scaped,
a concrete spirit where the grass is *ready*.
The landscape walks around in itself
like the luminosity in loom recasts
the miracle of how it all in fits.

DISTINCT

I was no longer the mother I had used to be,
nor had ever been. Five blue days
and one black one, or was it the five gray
and one clear one, a succession of blue and white
and gray and black ones. Refused the window.

I used to give birth to each hour. Now
the sky is ripped open. The wind doctors everything.
I find it compelling, spring dragged
from the ground, and who's screaming?
suffers the bud to open, a kingly sensation.

The possible shrinks to the eye of a needle.
I stitch the frantic leaves to paper
before they hit the ground, old game.
But distance doesn't change by season,
my trees no father for themselves in winter,

and at night I face the ceiling, the limit of the room
falling white, and whiter when I see it,
the ghost of something that deprives a body.
The bitch moon will not to enter on its change.
The sun is never beggar at my door.

What flaw to give? the structure of a fly-crack?
window fixed upon the fly deserts it?
Mornings I defect from rising, myself gradually
bear to where the bones insided. No more
a torn from I am, nor needing to be cause.

PRODUCTS, PROMISES

Call the sparrows in the yellow tree yellow.
They are brown. Call her hip the arc
of the day where it disturbs
the absolute surface of the bed.

The sparrows timbrel and tam-tam.
The sound of the highway is sadder than usual.
Inside me there are electrical impulses
birds' songs incite, others truck traffic fires.

Where shall we pin the—? A casket cart
grumbles down the sidewalk, product
of a red factory. An anachronism
is the clang of an iron bar

the flower man bangs to distinguish
his wagon wheels' rumble. An instinctive
silence blazes through bodies.
—blame or our hopes I wanted

to make a distinction among the vehicles
electrical dead and alive the yellow leaves
sings the sparrows fly internally her hip passes
zenith unabsolutes our days.

GENERALATIVE

Damp cold spring that won't relinquish
the blossoms from first yellow thrall of generation. A
    delicate largeish creature
probably deer have nipped her tulips and good clean mud
is what the season's wrought us. Ronald Reagan meant to
    be Bogart
but the gods wouldn't have it. The critique of pure reason
spelled out in sweet gum bristles on the lawn they cut too
    close leaving patches
of dirt that aches to walk on me in sympathy.
A chair in the road is perfect back to traffic.

The bad taste shrunken head remanded into basement
for the school kids' disappointment
replaces inadequate, a feeling for the future
where hope the angel's bat on fearful
contemplation nothing changes.
The woods are dark and deep, but the lid on the grill
    unspeakably open.
I was one of the three witches, a few moments, enough to
    get me started,
not as an object or pretty picture with a detour from what
    matters,
but an action, like lifting drink from table, or standing in
    the drizzle.
Feel how cold my leg is.

CHANCE PHOTOGRAPH

I see the smiles and return the tendency,
respect puts itself out always,
its viral tendency, replicated
in executions not depicted

and which I ain't guilty of
though I mistook the same simile.
Evil is the outward sign of grace
posed, above a crude grave.

TROUBLE WITH THE SUN

The sun is the breadth of a man's foot.
—Heraclitus

The sun arrested us.
How can I explain this, neither cardiac
nor legalistic, and like a cell
has beams of light through the bars
we had bars of light for the bed.

We had been taught to avoid it
saying a fault in us and
beyond reduced atmospherics
and a whole host of genetics
our ancestor worship.

It slid up the restless night's sheets
still as it moved, a wire and current
and this was what woke us, and lulled us
what caught us
it curved to the curve of our calves
and it was us.

CLOSEST OF SHOES

Black-tied, blond, uniformed . . . women?
The happy hour bedlam rang foreign,
our waitress we pondered, doppelgängered? Yet couldn't,
the second wrinkled, in time's one track
not possible. Our dead isn't healthy, scarred, New
Year toasting with hoisted gold champagne;
regard not memory's furious provisioning.

One comfort's finished. I'll have . . . Then some
imitation drink arrives and it's drunk.
Reach beyond, the pastor had implored,
the grief elf in the night will fabricate you shoes
from memory-skin to vanish in. You'll have the shoes.
But we're not Episcopalian. We sobbed. The music, faux . . .
Hawaiian? swelled saccharine, swabbed our dolor.
To sweet slumber we staggered, no guise for her getaway.
    Still,

morning, like a forgotten order, whumped
atop the bed. Who takes the blame? Day dawned on us,
another of its perfect fits. The body sheathed, seethed
in golden light, as in the night when shaded shells
and driftwood, glued lamp-like, ugly-honest,
interrupted the hand's ontological flailings:
hoping to hide, needed light, naked or not. Summing up:

I had thought she was the same person. Me too.
The memorial echoed, resurrectionless, through the forest.
Gone bird, dreamed song. In the end
"her own heart beat her" as we felt her,

"too fast for such shoes," and feeling forced
ourselves into them. A pair synthetic. Genuine leather.
Which still real, which excessive to wear?

SPACE IN NUMBERS

Lost in focus-thought like a moth
head deep in a flower I had yesterday
gray and brilliant. The birds sang to you not present
while I listened for the sound I was watching
20,000 leaves under as in the sea
submerged one is indoors and out, the answer
to the question of can we have one indigo bunting
on the dead man's twenty-seven acres
and another's dying mother's distant Philadelphia
says we hold beloved dog in box of ashes
because she was the one we witnessed
inside and out of the world that lives in.

TO WHOM IT MAY

One morning the forsythia tennis ball
neon yellow. April. To whom
to return it, this first smack/stroke?

What calculus. We never apprehended
zero on the approach to infinity-winter.
The stalk-continuum had stalked us naturally.

Listen, you said, to that angry bird.
That bird, I goaded, is angry inside us.
Meanwhile garden reality jaywalked across us,

accosting our sky with undemandables.
Our absence was, as the winter, reconcilable.
A shot flower. Shudder. Shower-clouds. God

gave us shoulders, though no one had said it.
The bush doubled under its yellow was as white
to the oppressed teapot tree, so we called it.

Like racket masters we stroked our foreheads, anvils.
Impossible, look-alike snow. It looked,
like a cat up a tree, as if we were living in the past,

our idea, of love, in this case, squaring
the undesirables into a court, color and squawks. We
    weren't
able to desire them, like we mean, or return.

WHOSE

The apples refuse to extinguish.

Green apples in the rain
and the no more sun
are the dwarf green sun
of an overgrown tree
selected for its dwarfness.
There's a pattern, like in stars
one sees an already ended kind.
The yesterday of beds
and shortened legs.

I claim the tree was tired, claim the apples
claimed the light, samed the sun
down. I claim it's not deliberate
for my opportune,
my harbored song.
Their yellowed green
sang the flesh was uncontainable,
correctly chartreuse, and variable color.
I claim
the flesh that's incontainable.

The morning consists
of what's gone and stamped
upon my face the sound
of zero apples.
What I can't stand is another
God-proof or human error.
The voice from the above parlor

is interrupted splat, the crack and the slap
of there goes another one crap
on the concrete exactly like a face
searched for its victimhood.

I laughed because my side
could split, because out in that
flesh splat I was spoken,
naturally bespoke.
But I admit my head's intact,
admit I got a hole to give,
pleading who's lost and whose apples,
and whose wasn't even his.

FAR OFF

That is hot ice and wondrous strange snow.
How shall we find the concord of this discord?
—Theseus, *A Midsummer Night's Dream*

The moon's white as a cut finger;
the road drives the car; I'm a spectator.
White dashes flash by, and the pine shadows
loom and retreat; it's arctic and mechanical,
primeval or eternal, the idea
of a beer at the bar with the locals.
The smoke curls around itself like an animal, a man
asks if we should have another
because for the last hour he's been lighting
Kools on the stool beside me. I'd wanted

to live alone for a while in the mountains,
but the town appeared inhabited,
an unlunar surface, the trees lit up
as with cheap electric colored lights.
The backyards harbored rivers, winding
like winding sheets behind covered porches.
The old man dead in the woods

was a tragedy and not a surprise. A spring drought
and a summer flood and a fall of rain.
Just this morning
the sun stopped rising, a cloud caught
in the pines showed its red lining
to the moon pearled, still high in the west,

as thunderheads heading north scraped the mountains
proclaiming brief rain and thunder, all in the half-hour
of my waking. Why

it seems of great constancy, strange and admirable,
everything double and like a jewel,
mine own, and not mine own? Because the mountains
far off turned into mountains—
you were far off—the clouds
into clouds.

HER FLORIDA

Artifice has limits. Cracked sidewalk, cracked face.

The roots don't like it any other way.

Domestic, wild, the ducks are dangerous matings.

Waddling along the man-made lake.

Their ruby heads raw as grapefruit pulp, their feathers
bleached to a semblance.

Hissing they will bite the hand forever of the child that
has fed them.

Home is just a place like this, where the sun makes
demands.

Pineapple in a swaddle of spiky leaves. The lizard's
monumental tail abandoned by the pool.

The ocean offers escape from beautiful beaches.

A cipher of fire ants and shrinking cruise ships.

Beads of sweat on the motel window, on the freeway, the
strip mall, the crescent moon.

The native nomad, naked on the bed.

Not generic, but specific, a point of impact, the cracks'
 star, the star's . . .

See how she flicks her severed tail, sheds the flood, raises
 her streamlined, partial, sickle self.

VISUAL INTERPRETATION

The wind evolves into the day the daffodils open it
the cloud are moved like leopards on canvas the still that
    motion
applies to objects the girl that dances then the camera
    becomes her
without a clear sense of who is sacrificed
the clatter in a bar of voices of dishes insistent
which is which of lipstick and hair clips
to the silence we have been for years discussing the lake
a man digs at the base of the street to float the house
in the hollow qualified laughter the curtain
pulled because the nights are cold like the folds of a column
opened no longer the woman has its own sensation
to stand and stare the ocean in its face is speechless
    enough
for what the wind had meant to spring to us

THIS ANIMAL

This animal
which lives two days and never
sees the sun, this animal the sun
has never seen, which would consume itself with seeing—
how did we call it?

The blood white,
and the knife boat
and the sea body—
all three were flying
indiscriminate into space
without a trace of logic
a roar in the aether
a reliable witness.

But the self is contained
and then again contained
and then a third time contained
to an utter deviation.

The dress we gave a character, white,
wore the size of our address. It was a shift
to absence, a seize, caesura, a scar
over cardinal,
a stepped into the cloud,
and found her air a substance.

This animal of where,
where the roots descend our negative,
we emerge inside an antidote.

Existence is the dirt
and root of double-giving,
until our displacement's always
is finely, faintly overthrown.

Dense planet, growth-riddled planet,
the seed consumed assumes a place
where hope trap, where horror flower
a need to give over and over
the address to the actual, the transparent curtain
never parted, her breath not taken, the warmth in
the form of this animal space

after two days taken.

EXCHANGE

Three fingers, three dollars. A bouquet harbors three pocked petals, black as dimples. The dog licks her corner to dream there. Without time and space, I can't imagine you (Immanuel Kant).

You kiss the air as it passes. I inhale the grave risk proved on three axes, three vases, thornless, flush with the meditative heads of cheap roses. The cysts fall away like an eyelash, touched from the face.

Hung by their heels the roses grow hard, archaic against the hall's white tile. Tomorrow, we step past essence on the way to breakfast. Time and space can be imagined without you. The petals are an admission,

crushed between fingers, red ash and a scent more bitter, like an emptiness when I approach you, too idol, to resist.

THE ANXIETY OF INNOCENCE

How could I walk away from what mattered
to me, to here where things matter to themselves?
The chimney smoke approximates the zither
of your hips so poorly, the birch leaves died yellow

above it, green elsewhere. On the roof
the rain flubs your name so incessantly,
the crows have only answers, stuck in the caw,
to pre-historic questions. Even the gold finch

is an evening grosbeak.
Several, actually. They feed in the grass,
get flustered, regroup. Their duplicity
is such blunt simplicity.

The deer tear wild thyme dispassionately,
regarding me. Alack my options.
Why aren't they bounding?
A whiff of exhaust here is alarming.

The anxiety of innocence extends
to my devotion isn't natural. But who needs lessons?
An orange coat speeds toward the center,
and the lake at each increment slips outward

away from itself, a futile description, feudal,
as if it could owe fealty. What I fear is,
fear is most itself in waiting,
and what when it arrives?

The hard frost we've heard predicted
we project will kill the flowers that haven't,
so kindly we stem them from themselves.
Invested or di-? It's not natural, the asking,

which preserves the beloved by fallacy
from it, nature disappointed unto. The coyote
lopes, keeping his own wary distance.
Where are you? plunges on, against the incipience of it all.

ECLIPSED

Let me propose to you this way.
From here to Canada, where the tundra
Offers the sky like bare flesh beside its bleakness,
During the latest eclipse
Retinas were burned, lines were crossed
That seemed like opposites until they bent space,
As touching you more and more suddenly wasn't,
Where the occluded sun, eyeball, and occluding moon
All take a role. Aw, one guy was stuck
Behind a milk truck in traffic. The stainless steel
Was protecting the milk, see.
The damage came undone like a ravel of hair
Which didn't belong to anyone.
Logic is furious.
Run a little faster, dame, demimonde.
I'll try to keep up
While my eyes ache in sympathy
With the dim shapes we used to call the world.
I can't say I'm sorry,
You who are to me both sun and moon.

Richard Meier was born in 1966 and raised in Duxbury, Massachusetts. He has worked with Teachers and Writers Collaborative as a writer-in-residence in the New York City public schools and as a teacher. His poems have appeared in *American Poetry Review*, *Boston Review*, *Chelsea*, *Fence*, *The Paris Review*, *Verse*, and other magazines. His first book of poetry, *Terrain Vague*, was selected by Tomaz Salamun as winner of the 2000 Verse Prize.

VERSE PRESS

Founded in 2000, Verse Press publishes eight to ten books per year. Its list includes not only poetry and prose by American poets, but work by English-language poets from other countries and poets writing in other languages. Guided by an editorial mission similar to that of *Verse* magazine, Verse Press is truly international, focusing on the innovative without ignoring tradition. In 2001, Verse Press will launch its First Books series, which will reprint first collections that have gone out of print.

www.versepress.org